MW01714529

FRESH & TASTY

Great value meals

R&R PUBLICATIONS MARKETING PTY LTD

Published by:
R&R Publications Marketing Pty. Ltd
ACN 083 612 579
PO Box 254, Carlton North, Victoria 3054 Australia
Phone (61 3) 9381 2199 Fax (61 3) 9381 2689
E-mail: richardc@bigpond.net.au
Australia wide toll free: 1800 063 296

Fresh & Tasty Great Value Meals

Publisher: Richard Carroll
Creative Director: Paul Sims
Production Manager: Anthony Carroll
Computer Graphics: Lucy Adams
Food Photography: Steve Baxter, Phillip Wilkins, David Munns, Thomas Odulate, Christine Hanscomb and Frank Wieder
Home Economist: Sara Buenfeld, Emma Patmore, Nancy McDougall, Louise Pickford, Jane Stevenson, Oded Schwartz, Alison Austin and Jane Lawrie
Food Stylists: Helen Payne, Sue Russell, Sam Scott, Antonia Gaunt and Oded Schwartz
Recipe Development: Terry Farris, Jacqueline Bellefontaine, Becky Johnson, Valerie Barrett, Emma Patmore, Geri Richards, Pam Mallender and Jan Fullwood
Nutritional Consultant: Moya de Wet BSc SRD
Proof Reader: Cindy Brown

Includes Index
ISBN 1 740221 265
EAN 9 781740 221 269

First Edition Printed June 2002
Computer Typeset in Times New Roman, Verdana, Helvetica, Shelley Allegro & Humanist
Printed in Singapore

CONTENTS

INTRODUCTION

Not even the all-powerful Computer Age has swallowed up people's love of the simple things in life - things such as the unrivalled aroma of homemade cooking after a tiring day at work. It's something that no gadget on the shelf of a multi-million dollar store chain or a trendy online ordering service will ever replace.

So the challenge to the everyday cook is to make their delicacies worthy to meet those lofty expectations without draining the bank account or sapping time from an already busy schedule. Great Value Meals fulfils those objectives with a refreshing abundance of ideas that will give you confidence to cover every meal occasion with ease.

We have divided this cookbook into chapters for quick reference, from Soups, Salads & Starters that will make you salivate right through to Desserts to die for-it's all within these pages. Our professional team has tested each individual recipe to deliver a straightforward, yet stunning, result. We dare you to try even one recipe because we are sure you will be addicted to your new 'gift' for culinary creativity.

SIMPLE METHODS STUNNING RESULTS

The beauty of this cookbook lies not just in its tantalizing images that tease your senses and make your mouth water, but the genuine promise that anyone can achieve these brilliant results. Our recipes utilize ordinary ingredients and state realistic preparation times so that there are no obstacles as you embark on the path to your new-found success. However, the results can be deceptive because your family and friends will think you have gone to a monumental effort to lay out before them a dish that looks wonderful, smells delectable and tastes nothing less than sensational. But who really needs to know any different?

To further simplify this process, we have included a glossary of terms and a section on weights and measures to take the guesswork out of your cooking. So keep this cookbook handy, because you never know when you will get the next opportunity to show your world food that is truly worthy of all its fanfare. After all, not everyone can be the top dog at work but they certainly can become king of the kitchen at home with Great Value Meals. Enjoy.

SOUPS, STARTERS & SALADS

Summon your creative energies with our choice selection of soups, starters and salads. Be the artist in your own kitchen, as your counter becomes your canvas, and your lunch, brunch or dinner guests your admiring fans.

You will explore the far reaches of your imagination as your mind meanders through each recipe, finding tantalizing soups, sensational salads and finger foods that will set the mood for the next course to come. What's more, with our expert tips, even the first timer can perform like a pro! We invite you to tap into that part of you that wants to entertain with artistic prowess and leave your family and friends begging to be the first to sample your next creation.

Serves 4 **Preparation** 30mins **Calories** 775 **Fat** 33g

MINESTRONE SOUP IN SODA BREAD

Ingredients

1 tbsp vegetable oil
6 rashers rindless streaky bacon, chopped
1 onion, chopped
2 cloves garlic, chopped
1.2litres/2pints vegetable stock
2 tbsps tomato purée
55g/2oz dried spaghetti
salt and black pepper

For the soda bread
225g/8oz wholemeal flour
225g/8oz plain flour
½ tsp salt
1 tsp bicarbonate of soda
55g/2oz chilled butter, cubed
2 tbsps chopped fresh parsley
juice of ½lemon
1 cup/250mL full-fat milk

1. Preheat the oven to 200°C/400°F Gas mark 6. To make the bread put the wholemeal flour into a bowl, then sift in the plain flour, salt and bicarbonate of soda, mixing well. Rub in the butter until the mixture resembles coarse breadcrumbs. Mix in the parsley. Add the lemon juice to the milk and stir into the flour mixture to form a soft but not sticky dough.
2. Knead the dough lightly on a floured surface and flatten slightly into a 20cm/8in round. Place on a baking sheet and cut a cross into the top. Cook at the top of the oven for 35-40 minutes, until well risen and golden.
3. Meanwhile, heat the oil in a large saucepan. Add the bacon, onion, garlic, carrot, leek and potato and cook for 5 minutes or until softened. Stir in the stock and tomato purée, then simmer, covered, for 20 minutes or until all the vegetables have softened. Break the spaghetti into 2.5cm/1in lengths and add to the pan. Cook for 10 minutes or until the pasta is tender but still firm to the bite. Season to taste and serve with the bread.

Photograph appears also on page 6

PARSNIP AND APPLE SOUP WITH GARLIC CROUTONS

Ingredients

2 tbsps vegetable oil
1 onion, chopped
2 parsnips, chopped
1 cooking apple, chopped
600mL/1 pint vegetable stock
2 tbsps chopped fresh parsley, plus extra to garnish
½ tsp dried marjoram
450mL/¾ pint full-fat milk
salt and black pepper

For the croutons
2 thick slices day-old white bread, crusts removed
1 large clove garlic, halved
2 tbsps vegetable oil

1. Heat the oil in a large heavy-based saucepan. Add the onion and parsnips and cook for 5 minutes or until softened. Add the apple, stock, parsley and marjoram and bring to the boil. Cover and simmer for 20 minutes or until the vegetables are tender.
2. Meanwhile, make the croutons. Rub both sides of each slice of bread with a half-clove of garlic. Cut the bread into 1cm /½in cubes. Heat the oil in a heavy-based frying pan. Add the bread and fry for 2-3 minutes, until golden, stirring constantly. Drain on kitchen towels.
3. Remove the soup from the heat. Stir in the milk and season to taste. Blend until smooth in a food processor or with a hand blender. Reheat and serve with croutons. Garnish with the parsley.

Parsnips and apples give this smooth thick soup a natural sweetness. Just serve it with chunks of crusty bread if you don't want to make the croutons.

Serves 4 **Preparation** 20mins **Cooking** 30mins **Calories** 293 **Fat** 17g

CHEFS AUTUMN SALAD

Ingredients

salt and black pepper
225g/8oz broccoli, cut into small florets
1 romaine lettuce, leaves torn
1 red onion, halved and sliced
12 cucumbers, peeled and diced
2 sticks celery, sliced
2 carrots, cut into matchsticks
2 apples, diced
200g/7oz wafer-thin cooked turkey or ham slices
2 tbsps each raisins and roasted salted peanuts, chopped (optional)

For the dressing
1 tsp Dijon mustard
juice of ½ lime
145g/5oz carton low-fat natural yoghurt
2 tbsps olive oil
1 tbsp chopped fresh coriander seasoning

1. Bring a large saucepan of salted water to the boil. Add the broccoli, return to the boil, then cook for 1-2 minutes, until slightly softened. Drain and leave to cool for 15 minutes. Meanwhile, make dressing. Mix together the mustard, lime juice, yoghurt, oil, coriander and seasoning.
2. Place the lettuce, red onion, cucumber, broccoli, celery, carrots and apples in a large bowl. Pour over dressing and toss to coat. Arrange turkey and ham slices in centre of a shallow serving dish or platter and spoon the salad around the edge. Scatter over the raisins and peanuts.

Serves 4 **Preparation** 30mins plus 15 mins cooling **Cooking** 2mins **Calories** 250 **Fat** 8g

Chef's Salad can have almost anything in it. This one makes good use of colourful fresh vegetables and apples, and comes with a zingy lime and coriander dressing.

Serves 4 **Preparation** 20mins **Cooking** 30mins **Calories** 353 **Fat** 20g

SALADE NICOISE

Ingredients

4 small waxy potatoes
225g/8oz fine green beans
3 medium eggs
4 tomatoes
12 white onions, thinly sliced
170g/6oz can tuna in oil, drained
8 black olives, halved
6 anchovy fillets (optional), halved
2 small lettuce, leaves separated
watercress sprigs to garnish

For the dressing
4 tbsps sunflower oil or olive oil
1 tbsp white wine vinegar
salt and black pepper

1. Boil the potatoes in a saucepan of salted water for 15-20 minutes, until tender. Drain and set aside until cool enough to handle, then dice. Meanwhile, cook the beans in another saucepan of boiling salted water for 5 minutes or until tender. Drain and halve.
2. Put the eggs into a saucepan of cold water. Bring to the boil, then cook for 10 minutes. Peel the eggs under cold running water and cut into quarters lengthways. Place the tomatoes in a bowl and cover with boiling water. Leave for 30 seconds, then peel and cut into wedges.
3. Place the potatoes, green beans, eggs, tomatoes, onion, tuna, olives and anchovies, if using, in a large bowl. Mix together the dressing ingredients, pour over the salad and toss lightly. Line a platter with the lettuce leaves and spoon the salad on top. Garnish with watercress.

No wonder Salade Nicoise has become so popular – it's colourful, healthy and delicious.

SPINACH AND CHICKEN OMELETTE BAGUETTES

Ingredients

4 medium eggs
½ tsp salt
1 tsp sugar
1 tbsp vegetable oil, plus extra for brushing
1 skinless boneless chicken breast, cut into very thin strips
1 clove garlic, crushed
225g/8oz fresh spinach, shredded
55g/2oz bean sprouts
2 tsps light soy sauce
4 small baguettes, cut in half lengthways

1. Break the eggs into a bowl, add the salt and sugar and beat lightly. Heat a 20cm/8in heavy-based frying pan and lightly brush with oil. Pour in a quarter of the egg mixture and swirl to coat the bottom of the pan. Cook for 1½ minutes or until the omelette is set and golden on the base, then turn over and cook for 30 seconds more or until cooked through. Remove from the pan and keep warm. Cook the remaining 3 omelettes in the same way.
2. Heat 1 tablespoon of oil in the frying pan, add the chicken strips and garlic, then cook for 3 minutes or until the chicken is cooked through. Add the spinach and bean sprouts and cook for 1-2 minutes, until the spinach starts to wilt. Sprinkle with soy sauce.
3. Top each omelette with a quarter of the chicken and spinach mixture. Roll up and place in a baguette, then serve straight away.

Serves 4 **Preparation** 15mins **Cooking** 15mins **Calories** 313 **Fat** 12g

Serves 4 **Preparation** 25mins **Cooking** 10mins **Calories** 541 **Fat** 18g

FALAFEL IN PITTA BREAD WITH SALAD

Ingredients

2 x 400g/14oz cans chickpeas, drained
1 small onion, finely chopped
1-2 cloves garlic, crushed
1 small red chilli, deseeded and finely chopped
½ tsp ground cumin
1 tbsp chopped fresh coriander
fresh lemon juice
1 medium egg, lightly beaten
3 tbsps plain flour
vegetable oil for frying
4 pitta breads, shredded lettuce, chopped tomatoes, Greek yoghurt and black pepper to serve

1. Blend the chickpeas, onions, garlic, chilli, cumin and coriander in a food processor to form a coarse paste, or use a hand blender. If the mixture is too dry to shape, add a little lemon juice.
2. Use your hands to shape the chickpea mixture into 20 balls, each about the size of a walnut. Dip into the beaten egg, then toss lightly in the flour. Heat 1cm/½in of oil in a deep heavy-based frying pan and fry half the falafel for 3-4 minutes, turning, until crisp and golden. Drain well on kitchen towels and keep warm while you cook the second batch.
3. Slice open each pitta bread, half fill with lettuce and tomatoes, then add 5 falafel. Top with a spoonful of yoghurt and sprinkling of black pepper.

These spicy little chickpea patties are the Middle East's most popular snack. They make a great filling for pitta bread, especially when topped with salad and yoghurt.

TERIYAKI CALAMARI SKEWERS

Ingredients

2 large calamari (squid) tubes, cleaned, cut into 5mm/½in thick rings

Teriyaki Sauce
1 shallot, thinly sliced
1 tsp minced fresh ginger
¼ cup rice wine vinegar or sherry
2 tbsps reduced-salt soy sauce
1 tsp honey
2 tbsps lime or lemon juice
1 tsp sesame oil

1. Soak 24 small or 8 large bamboo skewers in cold water for at least 20 minutes.
2. Preheat a barbecue or grill to a high heat.
3. Cut each calamari ring in half. Thread strips onto bamboo skewers in an 'S' shape - use 1 strip on small skewers and 3 strips on large skewers.
4. Place skewers on barbecue or under grill. Cook, turning several times, for 1-2 minutes or until calamari is just cooked.
5. Teriyaki Sauce: Place shallot, ginger, vinegar, soy sauce, honey and 1 tablespoon lime juice in a small saucepan over medium heat. Heat. Stir in sesame oil and remaining lime juice. Serve with skewers. If serving as a light meal, accompany with a tossed green salad. The skewers are delicious warm or cold.

Serves makes 24, 24 small skewers for a first course or 8 large skewers for a light meal - allow 2 skewers per serve
Preparation 20mins **Cooking** 5mins **Calories** 21 per skewer **Fat** 1g

Serves 4 **Preparation** 20mins **Cooking** 20mins **Calories** 292 **Fat** 5g

MOROCCAN LEMON CHICKEN SHISH KEBABS

Ingredients

510g/18oz skinless chicken breast fillets, trimmed of visible fat, cut into 2cm/¾ in cubes

Moroccan Lemon Marinade
1 tbsp chopped fresh parsley
1 tbsp fresh rosemary leaves or 2 tsps dried rosemary
2 tsps fresh thyme or 1 tsp dried thyme
1 clove garlic, crushed
1 tsp crushed black peppercorns
grated zest and juice of 1 lemon
1 tbsp olive oil

1. Marinade: Place parsley, rosemary, thyme, garlic, black pepper, lemon juice and zest and oil in a non-reactive bowl. Add chicken. Toss to combine. Cover. Marinate in the refrigerator for at least 30 minutes.
2. Preheat barbecue or grill to a high heat. If using bamboo skewers, soak in cold water for at least 20 minutes.
3. Thread chicken onto skewers. Place on barbecue grill or under grill. Cook, brushing frequently with marinade and turning, for 6-10 minutes or until chicken is cooked. Serve with Red Pepper Harissa for dipping.

Ingredients

900g/2lb lean pork schnitzel, trimmed of visible fat, pounded until very thin
2 granny smith, royal gala or braeburn apples, chopped
$^{1}/_{2}$ cup/60g sultanas
juice of $^{1}/_{2}$ lemon
$^{1}/_{2}$ cup/125 mL plum sauce
$^{1}/_{2}$ cup/125 mL apple juice
1 tbsp reduced-salt soy sauce
1 tbsp honey

PORK APPLE PARCELS

1. Preheat oven to 180°C/350°F/ Gas 4.
2. Cut pork into 10cm/4in squares. Set aside.
3. Place apples, sultanas and lemon juice in a bowl. Mix to combine. Spread each pork square with plum sauce to within 2cm/$^{3}/_{4}$in of the edges. Place a small mound of the apple mixture in the centre. Roll up to form a parcel. Tie with cooking string. Place in a casserole dish.
4. Combine apple juice, soy sauce and honey. Pour over pork parcels. Cover loosely with aluminium foil. Bake for 20-25 minutes or until pork is browned and tender. Remove parcels from casserole dish.
5. Stir 2 tablespoons plum sauce into cooking juices. Serve with parcels for dipping.

Serves 12 parcels **Preparation** 12mins **Cooking** 30mins **Calories** 177 **Fat** 3g

Serves 4 **Preparation** 25mins **Cooking** 1hr 45mins **Calories** 671 **Fat** 37g

CHICKEN AND LEEK SOUP WITH HERB DUMPLING

Ingredients

4 chicken thighs on the bone
1 onion, chopped
1 carrot, chopped
herb bundle made up of fresh tarragon, parsley and a bay leaf
55g/2oz butter
310g/11oz potatoes, cubed
3 large leeks, sliced
salt and black pepper
2 boneless skinless chicken breasts, cut into small pieces
2 tsps chopped fresh tarragon
140mL/5fl oz carton single cream

For the dumplings
100g/3½oz self-raising flour
30g/1oz fresh white breadcrumbs
55g/2oz shredded suet
3 tbsp chopped fresh herbs, such as tarragon, parsley or chives

With its generous portions and delicious herby dumplings, this creamy soup is almost a meal in itself.

1. Place the chicken thighs, onion, carrot and herbs in a saucepan with 1.5 litres/2¾ pints of water. Simmer, covered, for 1 hour. Strain the stock and skim off any fat. Finely chop the chicken, discarding the skin and bones. Heat half the butter in a saucepan. Add the potatoes and two-thirds of the leeks, cover and cook for 10 minutes. Pour in 1 litre/1¾ pints of the stock and season. Simmer for 10-15 minutes, until softened. Blend until smooth in a food processor, or use a hand blender, then stir in the cooked chicken.
2. To make the dumplings, mix together the flour, breadcrumbs, suet, herbs and seasoning. Stir in 4 tablespoons of water, then shape into 8 dumplings. Cook in simmering salted water for 15-20 minutes.
3. Meanwhile, heat the rest of the butter in a frying pan. Cook the chicken breast for 4-5 minutes. Add the remaining leek and cook for 2-3 minutes, until tender, then add to the soup with the tarragon and more stock, if necessary. Bring to the boil and simmer for 2 minutes. Remove from the heat and stir in the cream. Divide between 4 serving bowls. Drain the dumplings and add 2 to each bowl.

MEAT DISHES

Sink your teeth into a mouth-watering meat dish that is sure to make even the heartiest Texan steak lover go green with envy. We've smothered beef, pork and lamb in chopped vegetables and mixed seasonings to boast a bold new taste with every single recipe. Whether it's a Scottish-inspired Clapshot Pie or Mexican-style Beef Olives, not even national boundaries have stopped us from bringing you a world class culinary experience right here in the Land Down Under. Our national icon, Skippy the Kangaroo, is breathing a sigh of relief because thanks to our expert kitchen tag team we can offer you new taste twists on everyday meat.

So fire up your oven because it's going to be BIG!

YORKSHIRE PUDDING IN SAVOURY MINCE

Ingredients

115g/4oz plain flour
salt and black pepper
2 medium eggs
285mL/10fl oz milk
2 tbsps vegetable oil
1 onion, chopped
1 carrot, chopped
100g/3½ oz mushrooms, chopped
340g/12oz beef mince
200g/7oz can chopped tomatoes
200g/7oz baked beans
fresh parsley to garnish

1. Sift flour and pinch of salt into a bowl, then make a well in the centre. Break eggs into the well. Beat eggs gradually drawing in the flour and adding milk a little at a time until it forms a smooth batter. Cover and leave for 30 minutes.
2. Preheat the oven to 220°C/425°F/Gas 7. Heat 1 tablespoon of oil in a large heavy-based frying pan and cook onion and carrot for 5 minutes or until softened. Add mushrooms and cook for 2-3 minutes, then stir in beef and cook for 5 minutes or until browned. Add tomatoes and cook for 15 minutes. Stir in baked beans, heat for 5 minutes, season and keep warm.
3. Meanwhile, divide the remaining oil between 4 Yorkshire pudding tins. Place in the oven for 5 minutes or until the oil is hot. Pour in the batter and cook for 20-25 minutes, until risen and crisp. Place on serving plates, spoon in the mince and garnish with parsley.

Serves 4 **Preparation** 15mins plus 30mins standing
Cooking 35mins **Calories** 423 **Fat** 16g

Photograph appears also on page 18

These Yorkshire pudding cases are delicious with a variety of fillings – try them with chicken curry, meatballs in tomato sauce or a thick vegetable ratatouille.

Serves 4 **Preparation** 25mins **Cooking** 30mins **Calories** 472 **Fat** 21g

LAMBURGER PIZZA WITH ONION TOPPING

Ingredients

1 tbsp olive oil, plus extra for greasing
1 large tomato
255g/9oz lean lamb mince
255g/9oz fresh turkey mince
1 tsp mild chilli powder
1 tsp Italian herb seasoning
1 small egg
125g/4½oz fresh white breadcrumbs
1 onion, coarsely chopped
1 clove garlic, crushed
2 tsps caster sugar
½ tsp dried thyme
145g/5oz ball mozzarella, sliced

1. Preheat the oven to 190°C/375°F Gas mark 5. Lightly oil a 23cm/9in pizza tin or flan dish. Put the tomato into a bowl and cover with boiling water. Leave for 30 seconds, then drain, peel and slice.
2. Put the lamb mince, turkey mince, chilli powder, herb seasoning, egg and breadcrumbs into a bowl and mix well. Transfer to the pizza tin or flan dish and press with the back of a wooden spoon to cover the base. Bake for 25 minutes or until cooked through. Drain off any excess juices.
3. Meanwhile, make the topping. Heat the oil, add the onion and garlic and cook gently for 6 minutes or until softened. Add the sugar and thyme and cook for 10 minutes or until the onions have caramelised.
4. Preheat the grill to high. Spread the onions over the burger and arrange the mozzarella and tomato slices over the top. Grill for 3-5 minutes, until the cheese has just melted. Serve cut into large wedges.

A cross between a burger and pizza, this is sure to please children. They'll love it served with chips or mashed potatoes. You can make individual pizzas if you prefer.

Serves 4 **Preparation** 25mins **Cooking** 2hrs 35mins **Calories** 588 **Fat** 30g

LAMB HOTPOT COOKED IN CIDER

Ingredients

2 tbsps olive oil
4 loin lamb chops
6 lamb's kidneys, halved and skins and cores removed
1 onion, sliced
750g/26oz potatoes, sliced
2 carrots, sliced
1 large leek, sliced
2 sticks celery, sliced
salt and black pepper
3 sprigs fresh marjoram or oregano
300mL/10½fl oz dry cider

1. Preheat the oven to 180°C/350°F/ Gas mark 4. Heat 1 tablespoon of the oil in a large heavy-based frying pan. Add the chops and cook for 1-2 minutes each side, until browned. Remove from the pan, then add the kidneys and cook for 30 seconds on each side or until lightly browned.
2. Arrange half the onion and potatoes in the base of a casserole dish. Top with the chops; add half the carrots, leek and celery, then the kidneys. Add the rest of the carrots, leek and celery, seasoning each layer well. Finish with a layer of onions and potatoes, then tuck in the marjoram or oregano sprigs. Pour over the cider and brush the top with the remaining oil.
3. Cover and cook for 1½-2 hours, until the meat is tender. Remove the lid, place near the top of the oven and cook for 20-30 minutes, until brown.

SPICED LAMB AND APRICOT PILAU

1. Heat the oil in a large heavy-based saucepan and cook the onion, garlic and lamb for 5 minutes or until the onion and garlic have softened and the meat has browned. Stir in the turmeric, cumin, cinnamon and ginger, then cook for 1 minute, stirring, to release their flavours.
2. Add rice and cook, stirring, for 1 minute to coat well. Add tomatoes and half the stock, then stir in apricots and raisins. Cover and cook gently for 10 minutes, checking mixture from time to time and adding a little more stock if it starts to dry out. Add half of the remaining stock and cook for a further 10 minutes. Then add the rest of the stock and cook for 30-35 minutes, stirring, until the rice is tender and all the liquid is absorbed. Add a little extra water if the mixture becomes too dry.
3. Season to taste and remove from the heat. Cover and leave to stand for 5 minutes. Serve sprinkled with toasted almonds, if using.

In this dish, apricots, long-grain rice and tender chunks of lamb are simmered in a spicy stock. And it's all cooked in one pot so there's hardly any washing-up.

Ingredients

1 tbsp vegetable oil
1 onion, chopped
2 cloves garlic, chopped
510g/18oz neck of lamb or stewing lamb off the bone, cut into 2½cm/1in cubes
1 tsp turmeric
1 tsp ground cumin
½ tsp ground cinnamon
1 tbsp grated fresh root ginger
225g/8oz long-grain white rice
400g/14oz can chopped tomatoes
300mL/10½fl oz vegetable or lamb stock
115g/4oz ready-to-eat dried apricots, chopped
55g/2oz seedless raisins
salt and black pepper
3 tbsps toasted flaked almonds (optional)

Serves 4 **Preparation** 20mins plus 5mins standing **Cooking** 1hr **Calories** 654 **Fat** 28g

Serves 4 **Preparation** 20mins **Cooking** 1hr 40mins **Calories** 482 **Fat** 29g

SPARERIB CHOPS WITH RED CABBAGE AND APPLES

Ingredients

2 tbsps vegetable oil
4 large pork spare rib chops
1 onion, chopped
510g/18oz red cabbage, finely shredded
510g/18oz cooking apples, peeled, cored and thinly sliced
285mL/10fl oz red wine or vegetable stock
salt and black pepper
freshly flat-leaf parsley to garnish

1. Preheat the oven to 180°/350°F/ Gas Mark 4. Heat the oil in a large flameproof casserole dish. Add the spare rib chops and cook for 1½-2 minutes on each side, until lightly browned. Remove and keep warm. Add the onion and cook for another 5 minutes or until softened and golden.
2. Sir in the cabbage, apples and wine or stock. Season to taste. Place the pork chops on top and cover tightly. Cook for 1¼-1½ hours, until the pork is tender (you may need to add a little more wine or stock during cooking if the dish starts to dry out). Serve garnished with the parsley.

The sweet and sour flavour of red cabbage and apples is perfect with pork. Make sure you buy the meatier spare rib chops and not plain ribs. Serve with mashed potatoes.

MUSHROOMS STUFFED WITH PORK AND SAGE

Ingredients

8 very large open mushrooms or 16 open cup mushrooms
1 tbsp vegetable oil
1 onion, finely chopped
2 cloves garlic, finely chopped
170g/6oz fresh pork mince
145g/5oz fresh breadcrumbs
1 tbsp chopped fresh sage or parsley, plus extra leaves to garnish
1 medium egg, beaten
salt and black pepper

1. Preheat the oven to 190°C/375°F/ Gas 5. Remove any stalks from the mushrooms and finely chop. Heat the oil in a large heavy-based frying pan and fry the chopped mushroom stalks, onion and garlic for 3-5 minutes, until softened. Add the pork mince and cook for 5 minutes, stirring, until the pork browns.
2. Transfer the mixture to a bowl. Stir in breadcrumbs, sage or parsley and enough beaten egg to lightly bind the mixture. Season well.
3. Divide the stuffing between the mushrooms, using a spoon. Place on a baking sheet, bake for 20 minutes or until mushrooms have softened and the topping is golden. Scatter with the sage or parsley leaves.

Large mushrooms are crammed with a delicious mixture of herby pork and golden breadcrumbs. Serve with a salad and some lightly buttered new potatoes.

Serves 4 **Preparation** 20mins **Cooking** 30mins **Calories** 282 **Fat** 9g

Serves 4 **Preparation** 15mins **Cooking** 15mins **Calories** 622 **Fat** 20g

STIR-FRIED NOODLES WITH PORK AND GINGER

Ingredients

2 x 255g/9oz packs Chinese egg noodles
255g/9oz fresh pork mince
1 tbsp soy sauce
1 tbsp dry sherry
1 tsp cornflour
2 tbsps vegetable oil
2 spring onions, finely chopped, plus extra to garnish
1 tsp finely grated fresh root ginger
1 carrot, finely chopped
3 tbsps black bean sauce
150mL/¼ pint chicken stock

1. Cook the noodles according to the packet instructions, then drain well. In a bowl, mix together the pork, soy sauce, sherry and cornflour. Stir well to combine.
2. Heat the oil in a wok or large heavy-based frying pan, then add the spring onions and ginger and stir-fry for 30 seconds. Add the pork mixture and the carrot and stir-fry for 5-10 minutes, until the pork has browned. Stir in the bean sauce.
3. Pour in the stock and bring to the boil. Add the noodles and cook, uncovered, for 3-5 minutes, until most of the liquid is absorbed and the noodles are piping hot. Garnish with spring onions.

You can really smell the fresh ginger in this quick and easy Chinese dish. The sherry adds a little sweetness to the tangy sauce, which coats the pork and noodles.

A little beef goes a long way in this twist on chilli con carne. Serve it with bread or mashed potatoes.

MEXICAN-STYLE BEEF OLIVES

Ingredients

4 thin-cut beef steaks
4 rashers rindless streaky bacon, finely chopped
1 tbsp chopped fresh parsley
½ tsp dried marjoram
85g/3oz fresh breadcrumbs
55g/2oz flour
packet of cocktail sticks
salt and black pepper
1 tbsp vegetable oil
1-2 tsp hot chilli powder
1 onion, chopped
2 cloves garlic, finely chopped
1 red capsicum(bell pepper), deseeded and chopped
200mL/7fl oz beef stock
400g/14oz can red kidney beans, drained and rinsed

1. Preheat the oven to 150°C/300°F/ Gas 2. Place the beef between sheets of cling film and flatten slightly with a rolling pin. Put bacon into a large frying pan and fry gently for 2-3 minutes, until cooked. Remove from heat and stir in parsley, marjoram and breadcrumbs.
2. Mix together flour, salt and pepper in a shallow dish. Divide the bacon mixture between slices of beef, then roll up each slice from the short end, turn in seasoned flour and secure with a wetted cocktail stick.
3. Heat the oil in a flameproof casserole dish, add the beef and cook for 2 minutes, turning until browned all over. Remove from the dish and set aside. Add the chilli powder, onion, garlic and red pepper to the dish and cook for 3 minutes to soften. Return the meat to the dish, pour in the stock, and then bring to the boil. Cover the dish, then bake for 45 minutes. Add the kidney beans and cook for another 45 minutes. Remove the cocktail sticks and serve.

Serves 4 **Preparation** 20mins **Cooking** 1hr 45mins **Calories** 433 **Fat** 19g

Serves 4 **Preparation** 15mins **Cooking** 45mins **Calories** 427 **Fat** 32g

APRICOT AND CITRUS GLAZED CHICKEN

Ingredients

4 chicken leg joints, each about 255g/9oz each
1.2 litres/2 pints chicken stock
2 tbsps apricot jam
30g/1oz butter
finely grated rind of 1 orange and 1 lime or lemon
1-2 tsps light soy sauce

1. Place the chicken in a flameproof casserole dish, cover with the stock or water and bring to the boil. Lower the heat, cover and simmer for 35 minutes or until the chicken is cooked through.
2. Warm the jam in a saucepan for 1-2 minutes, then press through a sieve into a clean pan. Add the butter, orange and lime or lemon rind and heat for 1-2 minutes, until the butter has melted. Remove from the heat and stir in the soy sauce.
3. Preheat the grill to high. Remove the chicken from the poaching liquid and pat dry with kitchen towels. Remove the gristle from the end of each drumstick. Place the chicken in the base of a grill pan. Pour over the glaze and grill for 3-5 minutes, until golden brown and crisp.

Citrus fruits and a glaze of apricot jam give this gently poached chicken a sweet tangy flavour and a lovely crispy skin. Serve it with rice and shredded savoy cabbage.

DUCK WITH BRAISED TURNIPS

Ingredients

4 duck leg joints
510g/1lb 2oz white turnips, peeled and cut into 5cm/2in chunks
salt and black pepper
115mL/4fl oz chicken stock
1 tsp caster sugar
1 tbsp fresh orange juice

1. Preheat the oven to 190°C/375°F/ Gas Mark 5. Heat a non-stick frying pan, add the duck, skin-side down, then cook over a medium-high heat for 7-8 minutes, until browned. Pour off the fat that runs out and reserve. Place the duck, skin-side up, on a baking sheet and cook for 30-40 minutes, until the skin is crisp and the meat cooked through.
2. Meanwhile, cook the turnips in boiling salted water for 5-6 minutes, until softened, then drain. Place 2 tablespoons of the reserved duck fat in a large frying pan, add the turnips and fry for 5 minutes or until lightly browned. Add the stock and season.
3. Partly cover the pan and cook for 10 minutes or until the turnips are tender and almost all the liquid has evaporated. Uncover the pan, add the sugar and orange juice, then cook over a high heat for 3-4 minutes, stirring, until the turnips caramelise. Serve with the duck.

Serves 4 **Preparation** 15mins **Cooking** 50mins **Calories** 450 **Fat** 36g

Serves 4 **Preparation** 25mins plus 15mins standing **Cooking** 12mins **Calories** 230 **Fat** 10g

SKEWERED CHICKEN WITH SALSA

Ingredients

4 skinless boneless chicken breasts, cut into 2.5cm/1in cubes
¼ tsp Tabasco
1 tbsp olive oil

For the salsa
400g/14oz can chopped tomatoes
2 cloves garlic, crushed
½ red onion or 1 small ordinary onion, finely chopped
2 tsps mild chilli powder
salt
large pinch of cayenne pepper
1 tbsp chopped fresh coriander
1 tbsp olive oil
juice of ½ lemon

1. If using bamboo skewers, soak them in water for at least 10 minutes. Meanwhile, make the salsa. Place the tomatoes, garlic, onion, chilli powder, salt, cayenne pepper, coriander and olive oil in a bowl and mix together well. Cover and leave to stand for 15 minutes for the flavours to develop, then add the lemon juice.
2. Meanwhile, preheat the grill to high. Thread the chicken evenly onto 4 skewers. Mix together the Tabasco and oil and brush over the chicken. Grill for 10-12 minutes, turning often, until the chicken is cooked through and tender. Serve with the salsa.

You can make your own spicy Mexican salsa in minutes if you use canned tomatoes, and it really livens up these chicken kebabs. Serve them with tortilla chips.

Serves 4 **Preparation** 15mins **Cooking** 30mins **Calories** 439 **Fat** 20g

CREAMY CHICKEN KORMA

Ingredients

3 tbsps vegetable oil
1 onion, chopped
2 cloves garlic, crushed
3 tbsps plain flour
2 tbsps mild korma curry powder
750g/1lb 10oz skinless boneless chicken breasts, cut into 2.5cm/1in cubes
3440mL/12fl oz chicken stock
30g/1oz raisins
1 tbsp chopped fresh coriander
1 tsp garam masala
juice of ½ lemon
4 tbsps soured cream

1. Heat the oil in a large heavy-based saucepan, add the onion and garlic and cook gently for 5 minutes or until softened.
2. Put the flour and curry powder into a bowl and mix together. Toss the chicken in the seasoned flour, coating well. Reserve the flour. Add the chicken to the onion and garlic, then cook, stirring, for 3-4 minutes, until lightly browned. Stir in the seasoned flour and cook for 1 minute.
3. Add the stock and raisins and bring to the boil, stirring. Cover and simmer for 15 minutes. Add the coriander and garam masala and cook for a further 5 minutes or until the flavours are released and the chicken is cooked through. Remove the pan from the heat and stir in the lemon juice and soured cream. Return to the heat and warm through, taking care not to let the mixture boil.

If you like curry but don't want to spend hours in the kitchen, you'll love this. It's quite mild and goes well with rice or chapattis. Try it with crispy fried onion rings.

TURKEY AND MUSHROOM CREOLE

Ingredients

1 tbsp olive oil
1 onion, chopped
2 cloves garlic, chopped
1 red capsicum (bell pepper), deseeded and chopped
2 sticks celery, chopped
400g/14oz can chopped tomatoes
1 tsp chilli powder
large pinch of cayenne pepper
1 tsp paprika
¼ tsp dried thyme
455g/1lb quick-cook turkey steaks, cut into strips
115g/4oz button mushrooms, sliced

1. Heat the oil in a large heavy-based saucepan, then add the onion, garlic, red pepper and celery and cook gently for 10 minutes or until softened.
2. Stir in the tomatoes, chilli, cayenne, paprika and thyme and heat through for 1-2 minutes to release the flavours. Stir in the turkey strips and mushrooms, then cover the pan and cook gently for 30 minutes, stirring occasionally, until the turkey is cooked through and tender.

Serves 4 **Preparation** 20mins **Cooking** 45mins
Calories 198 **Fat** 5g

This West Indian-inspired dish tastes great and it's really healthy too. Serve it with some rice to soak up the spicy tomato and mushroom sauce.

Serves 4 **Preparation** 15mins plus 15mins standing **Cooking** 1hr 25mins **Calories** 607 **Fat** 45g

ROAST CHICKEN WITH SWEETCORN AND HAM FRITTERS

Ingredients

1 mini whole chicken, about 1kg/2lb 4oz
juice of ½ lemon
2 large cloves garlic, halved
1 small onion, quartered
salt and black pepper
1 tsp paprika
2 tbsps olive oil

For the fritters
2 medium eggs
4 tbsps full-fat milk
100g/3½oz self-raising flour
salt
200g/7oz can sweetcorn, drained
85g/3oz ham, finely chopped
vegetable oil for frying

1. Preheat the oven to 200°C/400°F/ Gas Mark 6. Rinse the chicken inside and out, then pat dry with kitchen towels. Sprinkle the inside of the chicken with lemon juice, then place the garlic, onion and seasoning in the cavity. Place in a roasting tin, sprinkle with paprika, then drizzle over the oil. Roast for 1-1¼ hours, basting 2-3 times during cooking. Check that it is cooked by inserting a skewer into the thigh; the juices should run clear. Rest, covered in foil, for 15 minutes before carving.
2. Meanwhile, make the fritters. Whisk together the eggs, milk and flour with a little salt until smooth. Stir in the sweetcorn and ham. Heat 5mm/¼in of oil in a deep heavy-based frying pan and drop in large spoonfuls of the mixture to make fritters. Cook the fritters for 1-2 minutes on each side, until crisp and golden (you may have to do this in batches) and serve with the chicken.

Succulent roast chicken is always a winner. But if you want to do something a bit different, serve it with these crunchy American fritters and some green beans.

PASTA WITH BACON AND CHICKEN LIVERS

Ingredients

2 tbsps vegetable oil
4 rashers rindless streaky bacon, chopped
1 small onion, finely chopped
1 clove garlic, crushed
225g/8oz frozen chicken livers, defrosted and chopped
2 tsps plain flour
170mL/6fl oz chicken stock
1 tbsp tomato purée
½ tsp dried marjoram
salt and black pepper
510g/1lb 2oz dried pasta quills (penne)
3 tbsps soured cream
chopped fresh basil or parsley to garnish

1. Heat the oil in a large heavy-based frying pan and cook the bacon, onion and garlic for 4-5 minutes, until softened. Add the chicken livers and cook, stirring, for 3 minutes or until they are starting to brown.
2. Stir in the flour. Gradually add the stock, stirring all the time. Stir in the tomato purée, marjoram and seasoning. Cover the pan and simmer for 10 minutes or until the chicken livers are tender and cooked through.
3. Meanwhile, cook the pasta according to the packet instructions, until tender but still firm to the bite. Drain well and transfer to a serving dish. Stir the soured cream into the sauce, then pour over the pasta and garnish with basil or parsley.

Serves 4 **Preparation** 15mins **Cooking** 20mins **Calories** 718 **Fat** 25g

Chicken livers, bacon and a little soured cream make a wonderfully rich and tasty sauce for pasta. But take care not to overcook the livers or they'll become tough.

Serves 6 **Preparation** 8mins **Cooking** 18mins **Calories** 335 **Fat** 8g

CHICKEN STROGANOFF

Ingredients

2 tbsps olive oil
1 onion, sliced
1 clove garlic, crushed
8 chicken thigh fillets or 4 boneless chicken breast fillets, sliced
115g/4oz button mushrooms, sliced
1 1/4 cups/10oz sour cream
1/4 cup/2 fl oz tomato pureé
1/2 tsp paprika
freshly ground black pepper
2 spring onions, chopped or chopped fresh parsley

1. Heat oil in a frying pan over a medium heat, add onion and garlic and cook, stirring, for 4-5 minutes or until onion is tender. Add chicken and cook, stirring, for 3-4 minutes or until chicken is just cooked. Add mushrooms and cook, stirring, for 2 minutes longer.
2. Stir sour cream, tomato pureé, paprika and black pepper to taste into pan, bring to simmering and simmer for 5 minutes or until sauce thickens. Sprinkle with spring onions or parsley and serve immediately.

Chicken is a cheaper choice for protein and works just as well as red meat in classic dishes such as this. Serve with rice or pasta and a green salad. If you prefer a saucier mixture, add a little chicken stock or a 440g/14oz can of undrained mashed tomatoes at same time as the mushrooms.

Photograph on page 41 opposite

APRICOT CHICKEN

1. Arrange chicken pieces in a large ovenproof dish. Scatter with onion, then sprinkle with soup mix and curry powder.
2. Combine apricots with juice and wine or water, pour over chicken and mix to combine. Cover and bake for 1-1 1/4 hours or until chicken is tender.

Chicken can be one of the least expensive bases for a main course, especially if you purchase the more economical chicken pieces such as legs, wings or thigh fillets.

Ingredients

1 1/2 kg/ 3lb chicken pieces
1 onion, sliced
45g/1 1/2 oz packet French onion or chicken noodle soup
2 tsps curry powder
440g/14oz canned apricot halves in natural juice
1/4 cup/60ml/2fl oz white wine or water

Photograph on page 41 opposite

Serves 6 **Preparation** 6mins **Cooking** 75mins **Calories** 325 **Fat** 2.5g

SEAFOOD DISHES

Ditch the soggy fish and chips at your local takeaway store, because we have put together a line-up of seafood dishes that bring all the goodness of the ocean right to your table. Seafood need not be the sole domain of the silver-service eatery when we give you the know-how to cook up a storm in your very own kitchen. Whether it's the spicy sensation of Tandoori Cod with Cucumber and Raita or the exotic excitement of Fresh Crab Tagliatelle, we are convinced that you will revisit this chapter time and time again. But why wait for a dinner party when you can enjoy these dishes on an ordinary day? Bon a petit!

Serves 4 **Preparation** 20mins **Cooking** 20mins **Calories** 218 **Fat** 10g

MOULES MARINIERES

Ingredients

2kg /4lb 8oz fresh mussels
2 onions, chopped
3 shallots, chopped
2 tbsps chopped fresh parsley, plus extra to garnish
145mL/¼ pint white wine or fish stock
4 tbsp double cream
salt and black pepper

1. Scrub the mussels under cold running water, then pull away any beards and discard any mussels that are open or damaged.
2. Put the onions, shallots, parsley, 150ml /¼ pint of water, and the wine or stock in a large heavy-based saucepan. Cook gently for 10 minutes or until the onions and shallots have softened. Add the mussels, then cover and cook for 5 minutes or until the shells have opened, shaking the pan from time to time. Place a colander over a bowl and strain the mussels. Reserve the cooking liquid and discard any mussels that remain closed.
3. Pour the reserved liquid into the pan and boil for 5 minutes or until reduced by half. Remove from the heat and stir in the cream. Season, if necessary. Return to the heat and warm through, but do not boil. Divide the mussels between 4 large bowls, pour over the sauce and sprinkle with parsley.

Photograph also appears on page 42

Fresh mussels with a cream and white wine sauce make a really impressive dish. Serve them with warm crusty bread to soak up the delicious juices.

These chunky fish cakes are packed with flavour and it only takes a few vegetables or a salad to make a complete meal. Canned salmon works just as well as the tuna.

TUNA, POTATO AND SPRING ONION FISH CAKES

Ingredients

4 slices bread, crusts removed
700g/1lb 9oz floury potatoes, such as King Edward, halved or quartered depending on size
3 tbsps mayonnaise
400g/14oz can tuna in oil, drained and flaked
1 tbsp chopped fresh parsley
2 spring onions, finely chopped
finely grated rind of ½ small lemon
3 tbsps plain flour
1 medium egg, beaten
vegetable oil for frying
lemon wedges to serve (optional)

1. Preheat the oven to 160°C/325°F/ Gas Mark 3. Place the bread on a baking sheet and cook at the bottom of the oven for 20-30 minutes, until crisp. Cool, break into pieces and crush with a rolling pin.
2. Meanwhile, cook the potatoes in a large saucepan of boiling salted water for 15 minutes or until tender. Drain, transfer to a bowl and mash with the mayonnaise. Leave to cool for 30 minutes.
3. Mash the tuna, parsley, spring onions and lemon rind into the potatoes. Flour your hands, then shape the mixture into 8 flat cakes. Dust with flour and dip into the egg, then into the breadcrumbs.
4. Heat 5mm/¼in of oil in a large heavy-based frying pan and cook the fish cakes for 3-4 minutes on each side, until crisp and golden (you may have to cook them in batches). Drain on kitchen towels, then serve with the lemon wedges, if using.

Serves 4 **Preparation** 15mins plus 30mins cooling **Cooking** 40mins **Calories** 681 **Fat** 36g

TANDOORI COD WITH CUCUMBER AND CARROT RAITA

Ingredients

145g/5oz carton natural yoghurt
1 tsp mild chilli powder
1 tsp paprika
1 tsp ground cumin
½ tsp ground coriander
½ tsp turmeric
1 tsp garam masala
1 large clove garlic, crushed
1 tsp tomato purée
juice of ½ lime
700g/1lb 9oz skinless cod fillet, cut into 4 pieces
¼ cucumber, grated
1 carrot, grated
145g/5oz carton natural yoghurt
2 tbsps chopped fresh mint or coriander

1. Mix together the yogurt, chilli powder, paprika, cumin, coriander, turmeric, garam masala, garlic, tomato purée and lime juice. Place the cod in a large, shallow, non-metallic dish. Pour over the marinade and turn to cover. Cover and refrigerate for 4 hours or overnight, turning occasionally.
2. To make the raita, pat dry the cucumber, using kitchen towels, and mix together with the carrot, yoghurt and mint or coriander. Cover and refrigerate until needed. Preheat the grill to high. Place the marinated cod in a roasting tin or shallow flameproof dish. Place under the grill and cook for 8 minutes or until the flesh is firm and cooked through, turning once. Serve the cod with the raita.

Serves 4 **Preparation** 20mins plus 4hrs marinating
Cooking 8mins **Calories** 209 **Fat** 3g

Tandoori spicing is a great way to liven up simple cod fillets. The raita is quick to make and adds a cooling contrast and a deliciously crunchy texture.

Serves 4 **Preparation** 20mins **Cooking** 1hr **Calories** 637 **Fat** 24g

There's something satisfying about making cannelloni, and this creamy filling certainly makes it worth the effort.

SPINACH, FISH AND RICOTTA CANNELLONI

Ingredients

340g/12oz cod or haddock fillet
255g/9oz dried lasagne verdi sheets
salt and black pepper
45g/1½oz butter
1 small onion, chopped
3 tbsps plain flour
425mL/¾ pint full-fat milk
1 tbsp snipped fresh chives or 1 tsp dried chives
juice of ½ lemon
225g/8oz frozen chopped spinach, defrosted, drained and excess water squeezed out
225g/8oz tub ricotta
1 tsp each chopped fresh parsley and basil, or ¼ tsp each dried
400g/14oz can chopped tomatoes
2 tbsps fresh white breadcrumbs
30g/1oz Cheddar, grated

1. Preheat the oven to 180°C/350°F/ Gas Mark 4. Place the fish in a large saucepan, cover with cold water and simmer for 10 minutes or until cooked through. Flake, discarding the skin and any bones. Cook the lasagne for 2 minutes in boiling salted water. Drain, rinse and pat dry with kitchen towels.
2. Heat 25g/1oz of the butter in a saucepan. Gently fry the onion for 4-5 minutes, until golden. Add the flour and cook, stirring, for 1 minute, then remove from the heat and slowly stir in the milk. Return to the heat, then bring to the boil, stirring. Add the chives, lemon juice and seasoning.
3. Heat the remaining butter in a saucepan, add the spinach and cook for 2-3 minutes, until wilted. Mix together the fish, ricotta and herbs, then fold in the spinach. Spoon a little mixture onto each lasagne sheet and roll up like swiss rolls. Arrange the tomatoes in a 25cm/10in square ovenproof dish. Place the rolls on top, pour over the sauce and sprinkle with breadcrumbs and Cheddar. Cook in the oven for 30-35 minutes, until golden.

Serves 6 **Preparation** 25mins plus 1hr 15mins cooling **Cooking** 1hr **Calories** 639 **Fat** 36g

SALMON KOULIBIAC

Ingredients

85g/3oz long-grain rice
2 medium eggs
1 tbsp oil
1 onion, finely chopped
1 tbsp chopped fresh parsley
55g/2oz mushrooms, finely chopped
juice of ½ lemon
salt and black pepper
385g/10oz pack ready-rolled fresh puff pastry
400g/14oz can salmon, drained and flaked
milk for brushing

1. Preheat the oven to 200°C/400°F/ Gas Mark 6. Cook the rice according to the instructions on the packet, then drain. Set aside for 1 hour or until completely cooled. Meanwhile, hard-boil the eggs for 10 minutes, then peel under cold running water and chop. Heat the oil in a frying pan, add the onion and cook for 5 minutes or until softened. Add the parsley and mushrooms and cook for 3-4 minutes. Stir in the lemon juice and season.
2. Roll out the pastry to extend the shorter side to 30cm/12in. Cut to make 2 rectangles, one 12x30cm /5x12in, the other 24x30cm/10x 12in. Place the smaller piece on a baking tray, prick with a fork and cook for 10 minutes or until lightly golden. Leave to cool for 15 minutes.
3. Combine the onion mixture, rice, eggs and salmon, then place down the centre of the baked pastry. Trim the corners from the unbaked pastry and lay it over the top. Dampen the edges, tuck under the pastry base and press to seal. Score the top, brush with milk and cook for 25-30 minutes, until golden.

This variation on a Russian pie uses canned salmon, but you could use lightly poached tail end fillets instead.

There's something satisfying about making cannelloni, and this creamy filling certainly makes it worth the effort.

FISH CAKES WITH TARTARE SAUCE

1. Cook the potatoes in boiling salted water for 15 minutes or until tender. Drain, then mash and leave to cool. Meanwhile, place the fish in a frying pan and pour over the milk. Cook over a low heat, partly covered, for 10 minutes or until just cooked. Remove from the milk and flake, discarding any skin or bones.
2. Mix together the fish, mash, parsley and spring onions and season well. Shape into 8 cakes, 2cm / 3/4in thick. Season the flour with salt and pepper. Dip the fish cakes into the seasoned flour, then the beaten egg, and finally the breadcrumbs, coating well. Refrigerate for 1 hour.
3. To make the tartare sauce, mix the mayonnaise with the crème fraîche, capers, gherkins, herbs, lemon rind and pepper.
4. Heat 5mm/1/4in oil in a frying pan and fry half the fish cakes for 5-6 minutes on each side, until golden. Drain on kitchen towels, then keep warm while you cook the rest. Serve with the tartare sauce.

Serves 4 **Preparation** 35mins plus 1hr chilling
Cooking 50mins **Calories** 726 **Fat** 43g

Ingredients

455g/1lb potatoes, cut into chunks
salt and black pepper
510g/1lb 2oz cod fillets
200mL/7fl oz full-fat milk
2 tbsps chopped fresh parsley
4 spring onions, finely sliced
4 tbsps plain flour
2 medium eggs, beaten
85g/3oz dried breadcrumbs
oil for shallow frying

For the tartare sauce
6 tbsps mayonnaise
2 tbsps crème fraîche
1 tbsp capers, rinsed, dried and chopped
2 tbsps finely chopped gherkins
1 tbsp chopped fresh parsley
1 tbsp chopped fresh tarragon
1/2 tsp finely grated lemon rind

VEGETABLE DISHES

Bland vegetables usually spring to mind when someone speaks of healthy eating - but why let your past experiences dictate your future encounters with these gifts from the garden when you know how to chop, sauté, season and do whatever it takes to ensure you never go back to boring? It's not just vegetarians who will find this chapter immensely useful, since we have gone to great lengths to ensure there is something for every palate. Discover how simple Asian greens can invigorate your taste buds or how the humble vegetable cheese bake can take on a whole new flavour. Try these recipes for yourself; they will become a daily habit welcome by even the strictest of dieticians.

Serves 4 **Preparation** 25mins **Cooking** 35mins **Calories** 352 **Fat** 20g

ROASTED VEGETABLES WITH MOZZARELLA

Ingredients

2 carrots, cut into matchsticks
2 small waxy potatoes, such as Charlotte, sliced
salt and black pepper
olive oil for brushing
1 red and 1 green capsicum (bell pepper), each deseeded and cut into 8 pieces
1 eggplant (aubergine), sliced
2 red onions, quartered
6 cloves garlic
145g/5oz ball mozzarella, grated

For the sauce
1 tbsp olive oil
1 small onion, finely chopped
2 cloves garlic, crushed
400g/14oz can chopped tomatoes
1 tbsp tomato purée
1 tsp dried oregano

This vegetarian dish is both filling and delicious; roasted carrots, potatoes, peppers and aubergine are served with a simple tomato sauce under a layer of melted mozzarella.

1. Preheat the oven to 230°C/450°F/ Gas Mark 8. Boil the carrots and potatoes in salted water for 2 minutes or until softened slightly, then drain.
2. To make the sauce, heat the oil in a heavy-based saucepan and cook the onion and garlic over a low heat for 5 minutes or until softened. Add the tomatoes, tomato purée and oregano. Bring to the boil, then reduce the heat and simmer, uncovered, for 20 minutes or until thickened.
3. Meanwhile, brush 2 large baking sheets with oil. Divide the carrots, potatoes, capsicum (peppers), eggplant (aubergine), onions and garlic between the sheets, arranging in a single layer on each. Brush with oil, season, then roast for 20 minutes or until softened.
4. Spread the tomato sauce over the base of an ovenproof dish and arrange the vegetables on top. Sprinkle with mozzarella and return to the oven for 5 minutes or until the cheese has melted.

Photograph also appears on page 52

Serves 4 **Preparation** 30mins **Cooking** 1hr 20mins **Calories** 477 **Fat** 31g

MIXED VEGETABLE CHEESE BAKE

Ingredients

1 large butternut squash, peeled, deseeded and cut into chunks
salt and black pepper
3 tbsps olive oil
1 large cauliflower, cut into florets
340g/12oz mushrooms, sliced
2 tbsps fresh white breadcrumbs
2 tbsps freshly grated Parmesan

For the sauce
30g/1oz butter, plus extra for greasing
30g/1oz plain flour
pinch of cayenne pepper
285mL/½ pint full-fat milk
1 tsp English mustard
100g/3½ oz Cheddar, grated

1. Preheat the oven to 200°C/400°F/ Gas Mark 6. Put the squash into an ovenproof dish, season, then drizzle over half the oil. Roast for 25 minutes, stirring once, until tender. Meanwhile, cook the cauliflower in boiling salted water for 5 minutes or until just tender. Drain, reserving 200ml/7fl oz of the cooking water, then refresh in cold water and set aside. Fry the mushrooms in the remaining oil for 4-5 minutes.
2. To make the sauce, melt the butter in a saucepan and stir in the flour and cayenne pepper. Cook for 2 minutes, then gradually stir in the reserved cooking liquid. Cook for 2-3 minutes, until thick, then gradually stir in the milk. Simmer, stirring, for 10 minutes. Remove from the heat, then stir in the mustard and the cheese, until melted. Season to taste.
3. Reduce the oven temperature to 180°C/350°F/ Gas Mark 4. Add the cauliflower to the squash, then divide between four individual ovenproof dishes. Scatter over the mushrooms and pour over the sauce. Mix the breadcrumbs and Parmesan, then sprinkle over each dish. Bake for 30-35 minutes.

Serves 6 **Preparation** 30mins plus 10mins cooling **Cooking** 1hr 15mins **Calories** 910 **Fat** 62g

POTATO, CHEESE AND ONION PIE

Ingredients

510g/18oz pack fresh shortcrust pastry
455g/1lb waxy potatoes, such as Charlotte, very thinly sliced
1 small onion, very thinly sliced
100g/3½oz Red Leicester, finely grated
salt and black pepper
145mL/5oz carton double cream

1. Preheat the oven to 180°C/350°F/ Gas Mark 4. Roll out two-thirds of the pastry on a lightly floured work surface and use it to line a 23cm /9in flan dish. Arrange the potatoes in a single layer over the base of the dish, then top with a layer each of the onion and Red Leicester, seasoning well between each layer. Pour over the cream.
2. Roll out the remaining pastry to make a lid. Lightly dampen the edges of the pie with water. Place the pastry lid on top and pinch the edges together to seal well.
3. Bake for 1-1¼ hours, until the potatoes and onions are tender. Leave for 10 minutes before serving to allow the cheese to cool slightly.

Waxy potatoes are best for this recipe because they hold their shape well. Serve the pie hot with lightly steamed savoy cabbage or cold with a crisp salad.

An easy yet very satisfying pizza! Adapt this recipe by using your favourite vegetables and cheese as a topping.

DEEP PAN VEGETABLE PIZZA

Ingredients

1 tsp dried yeast
340g/12oz strong plain flour
large pinch of salt
4 tbsps olive oil, plus extra for brushing and oiling

For the topping
225g/8oz can chopped tomatoes, drained
2 tbsps tomato purée
4 tsps olive oil
2 cloves garlic, crushed
20 fresh spinach leaves
115g/4oz button mushrooms, thinly sliced
1 red capsicum (bell pepper), deseeded and chopped
½ red onion, chopped
115g/4oz zucchini (courgettes), sliced
½ tsp each dried oregano and thyme
115g/4oz grated mozzarella

1. Put the yeast and 175ml/6fl oz of lukewarm water into a bowl and stir. Leave for 5-10 minutes, until frothy. Sift the flour and salt into another bowl and make a well in the centre. Mix in the yeast liquid and oil to form a dough. Knead for 5 minutes or until the dough is smooth and elastic.
2. Lightly brush a bowl with oil. Put the dough in the bowl, cover with oiled cling film and leave in a warm place for 1 hour or until it has doubled in size. Preheat the oven to 200°C/400°F/Gas Mark 6.
3. Knead the dough briefly, then roll out or press to fit a 30cm/12in loose-bottomed tin. Mix together the tomatoes and tomato purée, then spread over the base. Heat 2 teaspoons of the oil in a saucepan, add the garlic and spinach and cook, stirring, for 3 minutes or until the spinach wilts. Drain and arrange over the tomatoes.
4. Top the pizza with the remaining vegetables, herbs and mozzarella. Drizzle over the rest of the oil and cook for 30 minutes, until golden.

Serves 6 **Preparation** 35mins plus 1hr rising **Cooking** 35mins
Calories 566 **Fat** 21g

Serves 4 **Preparation** 30mins plus 10mins cooling **Cooking** 45mins **Calories** 364 **Fat** 25g

SWEET CORN AND MUSHROOM ROULADE

Ingredients

75g/2½oz butter, plus extra for greasing
115g/4oz mushrooms, chopped
75g/2½oz plain flour
145mL/¼ pint vegetable stock
115g/4oz canned or frozen sweetcorn, drained or defrosted
170mL/6fl oz milk
4 medium eggs, separated

For the pepper sauce
1 red capsicum (bell pepper), deseeded and halved
2 tomatoes
145g/5oz Greek yoghurt
1 tbsp chopped fresh coriander
salt and black pepper

Serve this light roulade and pepper sauce with a mixed salad, or on its own as an impressive starter.

1. Preheat the oven to 200°C/400°F/ Gas Mark 6. To make the sauce, roast the pepper for 20 minutes. Cool for 10 minutes, then skin and chop. Cover the tomatoes with boiling water and leave for 30 seconds. Peel, deseed and chop, then combine with the capsicum (pepper), yoghurt, coriander and seasoning.
2. Melt 15g/½oz butter in a saucepan, then fry the mushrooms for 3-4 minutes. Add 15g/½oz flour, stir for 1 minute, then remove from the heat and gradually stir in the stock. Return to the heat and simmer, stirring, for 1-2 minutes, until thickened. Add the sweetcorn and keep warm. Grease a 25x30cm/10x 12in swiss roll tin and line with baking paper.
3. Melt the remaining butter in a pan and stir in the rest of the flour. Cook for 1 minute, then remove from the heat and slowly stir in the milk. Bring to the boil, stirring. Cool slightly, then beat in the egg yolks. Whisk the whites until stiff, then fold into the yolk mixture. Pour into the tin, then cook for 15 minutes or until golden. Turn out and peel off the lining. Spread over the filling, then roll up and serve with the sauce.

Serves 4 **Preparation** 20mins **Cooking** 30mins **Calories** 182 **Fat** 5.7g

INDIVIDUAL MACARONI, BROCCOLINI AND CAULIFLOWER CHEESE

Ingredients

55g/2oz macaroni
255g/9oz cauliflower, cut into florets
255g/9oz broccolini or broccoli, cut into florets
1½ tbsps canola spread
1 tbsp plain flour
pinch saffron
pinch nutmeg
225mL/8fl oz reduced fat evaporated milk
⅓ cup grated reduced fat cheddar cheese

1. Preheat oven to 200°C/400°F. Lightly grease four 250ml ramekins (ceramic ovenproof dishes).
2. Cook the macaroni in a large pot of rapidly boiling water until al dente (cooked, but still with a bite to it). Drain well and set aside.
3. Steam or microwave the cauliflower and broccolini or broccoli separately until tender. Rinse under cold water and drain well.
4. Heat the canola spread in a small pot, add the flour, saffron and nutmeg and cook, stirring constantly, until bubbling. Remove from the heat and gradually stir in the milk.
5. Return the pot to the heat and bring to the boil, stirring constantly until the sauce boils and thickens. Reduce the heat and simmer for 5 minutes.
6. Put the macaroni in the base of the ramekins, top with the combined cauliflower and broccolini and pour over the sauce. Sprinkle with cheese. Bake for 15 minutes or until the sauce is golden and bubbling.

Serves 4-6 **Preparation** 15mins **Cooking** 15mins **Calories** 39 **Fat** 0.7g

BABY EGGPLANT WITH GINGER AND SWEET SOY

Ingredients

8 slender eggplant (aubergine)
canola cooking spray
3 cloves garlic, crushed
1 tbsp grated fresh ginger
1 tsp cumin seeds
pinch chilli powder
1 tbsp kecap manis
(sweet soy sauce)
2 tbsps lemon juice
¼ cup Thai basil leaves

1. Cut the eggplants in half, leaving the stems attached. Spray the cut sides lightly with the canola spray.
2. Heat a large non stick fry pan over a medium heat and add the eggplants, cut side down, and cook until they start to soften and turn golden. Remove.
3. Add the garlic, ginger, cumin, chilli powder and 1 tablespoon water to the pan and cook until the garlic is soft.
4. Stir in the kecap manis, lemon juice and 125ml water and bring to a low simmer. Return the eggplant to the pan and cook for 10 minutes or until soft and most of the liquid has been absorbed. Transfer to serving plates and top with Thai basil leaves.

ASIAN GREENS WITH SWEET SOY AND SESAME DRESSING

Ingredients

510g/18oz baby bok choy
510g/18oz Chinese broccoli
285g/10oz water spinach
½ tsp sesame oil
1 tbsp oyster sauce
1 tbsp kecap manis (sweet soy sauce)
1 tbsp rice vinegar
1 tbsp sesame seeds, toasted

1. Cut the bok choy, Chinese broccoli and water spinach into 20cm lengths. Wash, drain and put in a large bamboo steamer lined with baking paper. Cook over a wok of simmering water, making sure the base of the steamer does not come in contact with the water, for 5 minutes or until bright green and tender.
2. Whisk together the sesame oil, oyster sauce, kecap manis and rice vinegar in a jug.
3. Neatly pile the vegetables onto a serving plate and drizzle with the sauce. Sprinkle with sesame seeds and serve.

Serves 4 **Preparation** 5mins **Cooking** 5mins **Calories** 113 **Fat** 3.9g

Serves 4-6 **Preparation** 15mins **Cooking** 45mins **Calories** 243 **Fat** 6.6g

CREAMY POTATO GRATIN

Ingredients

750g/26oz waxy potatoes (desiree or sebago)
1 onion, thinly sliced
370mL/13fl oz reduced fat evaporated milk
115mL/4fl oz reduced salt chicken stock
½ cup grated reduced fat Cheddar cheese

1. Preheat the oven to 180°C/350°F. Peel the potatoes and cut into thin slices. Layer the potato and onion in a 6 cup capacity ovenproof dish.
2. Whisk together the evaporated milk, chicken stock and half the cheese. Pour over the layered potato.
3. Sprinkle with the grated cheese and bake, covered, for 30 minutes then uncovered for 15 minutes or until the potato is tender and the cheese is golden.

Serves 4 **Preparation** 10mins **Cooking** 10mins **Calories** 146 **Fat** 12g

MIXED BEANS WITH PINE NUTS AND PARMESAN

Ingredients

255g/9oz yellow beans, trimmed
200g/7oz green beans, trimmed
2 tbsps red wine vinegar
1 tsp honey
1 clove garlic, crushed
2 tbsps fresh mint, finely sliced
1 tbsp mustard seed oil
2 tbsps pine nuts, toasted
2 tbsps shaved parmesan
cracked black pepper to taste

1. Steam or microwave the beans until tender. Do not overcook or they will lose their colour. Drain well.
2. Whisk together the red wine vinegar, honey, garlic, mint and mustard seed oil in a small jug.
3. Pour the dressing over the beans and top with the toasted pine nuts, parmesan and cracked black pepper.

DESSERTS

From the chocolate-loving court of ancient Montezuma to the sugar-soaked cane fields of modern-day Queensland, the world has an undying devotion to all things sweet. With the passing of centuries has come great inventiveness in finding new facets for the best-loved course of them all, dessert. We have compiled a wonderful selection of treats that will flood your kitchen with untold delights, from the dumpling to the tart, the pudding to the crumble. Even a quick browse through these pages will prove to be a delightful journey into the senses. Don't settle for a simple scoop of ice cream or a packaged cake for dessert anymore when you can bring heaven to earth with your very own hands.

Serves 6 **Preparation** 20mins plus 30mins chilling **Cooking** 1hr 15mins **Calories** 751 **Fat** 49g

BAKEWELL TART WITH PLUMS

Ingredients

170g/6oz plain flour
45g/1½ oz icing sugar
85g/3oz butter, diced
1 medium egg yolk
juice of ½ lemon

For the filling
455g/1lb plums, halved, stoned and chopped
170g/6oz caster sugar
115g/4oz unsalted butter, softened
2 medium eggs, beaten
145g/5oz ground almonds
few drops almond extract (optional)
55g/2oz flaked almonds

1. Sift the flour and icing sugar into a bowl, add the butter and rub in using your fingertips until the mixture resembles fine breadcrumbs. Add the egg yolk and lemon juice and mix to a dough. Cover and refrigerate for 30 minutes.
2. Preheat the oven to 190°C/375°F/ Gas Mark 5. Use the pastry to line a deep 20cm/8in metal flan tin. Line with baking paper and baking beans, then bake blind for 10-12 minutes, until the pastry is golden. Set aside, then reduce the oven temperature to 180°C/350°F/Gas Mark 4.
3. Cook the plums with 50g/2oz of sugar in a saucepan for 10 minutes or until soft. Cool, drain, discarding the syrup, then spread over the pastry case. Beat the butter and remaining sugar together, until light and fluffy. Beat in the eggs a little at a time, then beat in the ground almonds and extract if using. Smooth the filling over the plums, sprinkle with the flaked almonds, then bake for 50 minutes or until the filling is set.

Photograph also appears on page 64

This tart was originally known as Bakewell pudding and it proves that old-fashioned things are sometimes the best.

APPLE DUMPLINGS WITH BUTTERSCOTCH SAUCE

Ingredients

510g/18oz pack fresh puff or shortcrust pastry
30g/1oz shelled pecans, chopped
30g/1oz stoned dates, finely chopped
½ tsp ground cinnamon
6 eating apples, such as Cox's, peeled
1 small egg yolk, beaten with 2 tbsp milk

For the sauce
85g/3oz butter
145g/5oz light muscovado sugar
145mL/5fl oz carton double cream
lemon juice to taste

1. To make the sauce, place the butter, sugar and cream in a heavy-based saucepan and stir until the butter melts. Boil for 2-3 minutes, until thickened, then add lemon juice to taste. Set aside.
2. Roll out the pastry on a lightly floured surface and cut out 6 circles just large enough to enclose the apples. Cut some leaves from the trimmings for decoration. Place the circles on a baking sheet.
3. Combine the pecans, dates and cinnamon with 6 tablespoons of the sauce. Cut out the centre of each apple to remove the core. Put an apple on each pastry circle, then half-fill with the pecan mixture. Gather up the pastry, brush the edges with egg mixture and pinch together, then brush all over with the egg mixture and decorate with the reserved pastry leaves. Refrigerate for 1 hour.
4. Preheat the oven to 190°C/375°F/ Gas Mark 5. Bake for 35-45 minutes, until the pastry is golden and the apples are tender. Gently reheat the remaining sauce and serve with the apples.

Serves 6 **Preparation** 30mins plus 1hr chilling **Cooking** 50mins **Calories** 770 **Fat** 50g

TREACLE TART

Ingredients

255g/9oz shortcrust pastry, defrosted if frozen
455g/16oz can golden syrup
100g/3½oz fresh white breadcrumbs
1 tsp ground ginger
finely grated rind of 1 lemon and juice of ½ lemon
2 eating apples, such as Cox's, peeled, cored and coarsely grated

1. Preheat the oven to 190°C/375°F/ Gas Mark 5. Roll out the pastry on a lightly floured surface and use to line a 20cm/8in flan tin at least 2.5cm/1in deep. Trim off the excess pastry and reserve for decoration. Line with baking paper and baking beans, then bake blind for 10-12 minutes, until the pastry is lightly golden. Remove the paper and beans.
2. Meanwhile, make the filling. Open the can of syrup and place in a saucepan. Pour in boiling water to reach halfway up the tin. Warm over a low heat for 5 minutes or until the syrup is very runny. Place the breadcrumbs, ginger, lemon rind and juice and apples in a bowl. Pour over the syrup and mix.
3. Pour the mixture into the pastry case. Roll out the reserved pastry and cut into strips, then twist gently. Lay the strips in a criss-cross pattern on top of the tart. Bake for 25-30 minutes, until bubbling.

Treacle tart has been a British favourite for centuries. Golden syrup is used rather than treacle these days, but the pudding has kept its name. Serve with vanilla ice cream.

Serves 6 **Preparation** 15mins **Cooking** 40mins **Calories** 487 **Fat** 12g

Serves 4 **Preparation** 25mins plus 5mins cooling **Cooking** 1hrs 30mins **Calories** 748 **Fat** 36g

GINGER AND PEAR STEAMED PUDDING

Ingredients

145g/5oz butter, softened, plus extra for greasing
145g/5oz light muscovado sugar, plus 1 tbsp to coat
3 ripe pears, peeled and cored, 1 chopped, 2 sliced
3 pieces preserved stem ginger, chopped, and 5 tbsps syrup from the jar
2 large eggs, beaten
170g/6oz self-raising flour
2 tsps ground ginger
30g/1oz fresh white breadcrumbs
finely grated rind of 1 lemon

1. Grease a 1.2 litre/2 pint pudding basin with butter and coat with 1 tablespoon of sugar. Carefully line the base and sides of the basin with the pear slices, then drizzle over half the ginger syrup.
2. Beat together the butter and sugar until light and fluffy, then gradually beat in the eggs. Sift together the flour and ground ginger, then fold into the butter mixture. Stir in the breadcrumbs, lemon rind, remaining syrup, the stem ginger and the chopped pear. Spoon into the basin and level the top, then cover the basin with a double layer each of baking paper and foil. Tie a piece of string around the rim of the basin to hold the layers in place, then cut off any excess paper and foil.
3. Place the basin in a saucepan and pour in boiling water to reach halfway up the basin. Bring back to the boil, then simmer, covered, for 1½ hours, adding more water as necessary. Remove the basin from the water and leave to cool for 5 minutes. Invert onto a plate, tap the base and remove the basin.

Serves 4 **Preparation** 15mins **Cooking** 45mins **Calories** 583 **Fat** 34g

RHUBARB AND STRAWBERRY CRUMBLE

Ingredients

510g/1lb 2oz rhubarb, cut into chunks
255g/9oz strawberries, hulled and halved
55g/2oz soft light brown sugar

For the topping
145g/5oz plain flour
pinch of salt
55g/2oz caster or soft light brown sugar
85g/3oz unsalted butter, cubed
85g/3oz ground almonds
55g/2oz slivered or flaked almonds

1. Preheat the oven to 180°C/350°F/ Gas Mark 4. Mix together the rhubarb, strawberries and sugar. Transfer to a 20x30cm/8x12in ovenproof dish.
2. To make the topping, sift the flour and salt into a bowl, then stir in the caster or brown sugar. Rub the butter into the mixture using your fingertips until it resembles fine breadcrumbs. Stir in the ground and slivered almonds, then sprinkle the mixture over the fruit.
3. Bake for 40-45 minutes, until the fruit juices are bubbling and the topping is lightly browned.

Almonds give this crumble its extra richness. It can be eaten hot or cold, with some lightly whipped cream, thick Greek yogurt or plenty of homemade custard.

THE EASIEST EVER APPLE PIE

Ingredients

255g/9oz plain flour
115g/4oz butter, cubed
2 tbsp apricot jam
455g/1lb cooking apples, peeled, cored and thinly sliced
1 tsp ground cinnamon
½ tsp mixed spice
finely grated rind of 1 orange
55g/2oz soft light brown sugar
55g/2oz sultanas
Icing sugar to dust

1. Preheat the oven to 190°C/375°F/ Gas Mark 5. Put the flour into a bowl and rub in the butter until the mixture resembles fine breadcrumbs. Add enough cold water (about 3-4 tablespoons) to make a smooth dough. Knead very lightly.
2. Roll out the pastry to 35cm /14in round on a lightly floured surface. Place on a large baking sheet. Spread the jam over the centre of the pastry. In a bowl, toss together the apples, cinnamon, mixed spice, grated orange rind, sugar and sultanas, then pile the mixture into the middle of the pastry. Bring the edges of the pastry up over the apple mixture, pressing into rough pleats but leaving the centre of the pie open.
3. Bake for 35-45 minutes, until the pastry is golden, covering the pie with foil if the apple starts to burn. Remove the foil, if using, then sprinkle over the icing sugar before serving.

Serves 4 **Preparation** 25mins
Cooking 45mins **Calories** 592 **Fat** 27g

This apple pie is a dream to make – there's no tin, so you don't have to fit the pastry and you needn't worry about it shrinking. Serve hot with scoops of vanilla ice cream.

GOLDEN OATY APPLE PUDDING

Ingredients

155g/5oz butter, plus extra for greasing
700g/1lb 9oz cooking apples, peeled, cored and chopped
200g/7oz ready-to-eat dried apricots, chopped
2 tbsps raisins
55g/2oz sugar
4 tbsps golden syrup
1-2 tsp finely grated fresh root ginger
255g/9oz rolled oats

1. Preheat the oven to 190°C/375°F/ Gas Mark 5. Butter a 20cm/8in shallow ovenproof dish.
2. Place the apples, apricots, raisins, half the sugar and 1-2 tablespoons of water in a saucepan. Cover the pan, then cook over a low heat for 10-15 minutes, until the apples soften, stirring occasionally, then set aside.
3. Heat the remaining sugar with the butter, golden syrup and ginger in a saucepan for 1-2 minutes, until the sugar dissolves, then stir in the oats. Add three-quarters of the mixture to the dish, using a wooden spoon to spread it evenly over the base and sides. Smooth the fruit mixture on top, then spoon over the remaining oat mixture and press down lightly with the back of the spoon. Cook for 30 minutes or until the top is golden.

Fresh root ginger gives this apple pudding a deeper and far more pungent taste than its ground equivalent and it complements the fruity filling perfectly.

Serves 4 **Preparation** 15mins
Cooking 50mins **Calories** 804
Fat 37g

Serves 4 **Preparation** 10mins plus 1hr 10mins **Cooking** 40mins **Calories** 468 **Fat** 21g

LEMON MERINGUE RICE PUDDING

Ingredients

85g/3oz pudding rice
570mL/1 pint full-fat milk
100g/3½oz caster sugar
2 strips of lemon rind, pared with a vegetable peeler
145mL/5fl oz carton whipping cream
100g/3½oz lemon curd
1 packet easy dried egg white

1. Put the rice, milk, 15g/½oz of the sugar and the lemon rind into a saucepan. Bring to the boil, then reduce the heat and simmer, uncovered, for 30 minutes until thick and creamy, stirring from time to time. Remove the lemon rind and set the rice aside for 1 hour or until completely cooled, stirring occasionally.
2. Preheat the oven to 200°C/400°F/ Gas Mark 6. Whisk the cream until it forms soft peaks, then fold into the rice. Spread the lemon curd over the base of a 9 x 6in/23x15cm ovenproof dish. Spread the rice on top. Whisk the egg powder and 50ml/2fl oz of water together until foamy (this is easiest with an electric whisk). Gradually whisk in the remaining sugar until thick and glossy. Spoon over the rice.
3. Cook at the top of the oven for 10 minutes or until the meringue is crisp and golden brown. Leave to cool for 10 minutes before serving.

Creamy rice pudding and sweet lemon curd are topped with a crisp, crunchy meringue. This pudding can be eaten hot, but it's even better served chilled.

FRUITY FRESH PLUM TOASTIES

Ingredients

4 thick slices fruit bread, brioche, cinnamon bread or chollah
1-2 tbsps plum jam
¼ tsp ground cinnamon
30g/1oz caster sugar
8-12 ripe red plums, halved and stoned

1. Preheat the grill to high. Toast the bread slices very lightly on both sides. Spread one side of the toast with the jam, then place the slices in a single layer in a flameproof dish, jam-side up.
2. Mix together the cinnamon and sugar. Arrange the plums on top of the toast and sprinkle with the cinnamon sugar. Place under the grill and cook for 2-3 minutes, until the sugar begins to melt and the plums are warmed through. Leave to cool slightly before serving.

Serves 4
Preparation 10mins
Cooking 5mins
Calories 211
Fat 4g

This is a great way of using up some leftover fruit bread. Use any soft fruit with its matching jam, if possible. Serve with a dollop of Greek yoghurt or crème fraîche.

GLOSSARY

acidulated water:
water with added acid, such as lemon juice or vinegar, which prevents discoloration of ingredients, particularly fruit or vegetables. The proportion of acid to water is 1 teaspoon per 300ml.
al dente: Italian cooking term for ingredients that are cooked until tender but still firm to the bite; usually applied to pasta.
americaine: method of serving seafood - usually lobster and monkfish - in a sauce flavoured with olive oil, aromatic herbs, tomatoes, white wine, fish stock, brandy and tarragon.
anglaise: cooking style for simple cooked dishes such as boiled vegetables. Assiette anglaise is a plate of cold cooked meats.
antipasto: Italian for "before the meal", it denotes an assortment of cold meats, vegetables and cheeses, often marinated, served as an hors d'oeuvre. A typical antipasto might include salami, prosciutto, marinated artichoke hearts, anchovy fillets, olives, tuna fish and Provolone cheese.
au gratin: food sprinkled with breadcrumbs, often covered with cheese sauce and browned until a crisp coating forms.
balsamic vinegar: a mild, extremely fragrant, wine-based vinegar made in northern Italy. Traditionally, the vinegar is aged for at least seven years in a series of casks made of various woods.
baste: to moisten food while it is cooking by spooning or brushing on liquid or fat.
baine marie: a saucepan standing in a large pan which is filled with boiling water to keep liquids at simmering point. A double boiler will do the same job.
beat: to stir thoroughly and vigourously.
beurre manie: equal quantities of butter and flour kneaded together and added a little at a time to thicken a stew or casserole.
bird: see paupiette.
blanc: a cooking liquid made by adding flour and lemon juice to water in order to keep certain vegetables from discolouring as they cook.
blanch: to plunge into boiling water and then, in some cases, into cold water. Fruits and nuts are blanched to remove skin easily.
blanquette: a white stew of lamb, veal or chicken, bound with egg yolks and cream and accompanied by onion and mushrooms.
blend: to mix thoroughly.
bonne femme: dishes cooked in the traditional French "housewife" style. Chicken and pork bonne femme are garnished with bacon, potatoes and baby onion; fish bonne femme with mushrooms in a white wine sauce.
bouquet garni: a bunch of herbs, usually consisting of sprigs of parsley, thyme, marjoram, rosemary, a bay leaf, peppercorns and cloves, tied in muslin and used to flavour stews and casseroles.
braise: to cook whole or large pieces of poultry, game, fish, meat or vegetables in a small amount of wine, stock or other liquid in a closed pot. Often the main ingredient is first browned in fat and then cooked in a low oven or very slowly on top of the stove. Braising suits tough meats and older birds and produces a mellow, rich sauce.
broil: The American term for grilling food.
brown: cook in a small amount of fat until brown.
burghul (also bulgur): a type of cracked wheat, where the kernels are steamed and dried before being crushed.
buttered: to spread with softened or melted butter.
butterfly: to slit a piece of food in half horizontally, cutting it almost through so that when opened it resembles butterfly wings. Chops, large prawns and thick fish fillets are often butterflied so that they cook more quickly.
buttermilk: a tangy, low-fat cultured milk product whose slight acidity makes it an ideal marinade base for poultry.
calzone: a semicircular pocket of pizza dough, stuffed with meat or vegetables, sealed and baked.
caramelise: to melt sugar until it is a golden brown syrup.
champignons: small mushrooms, usually canned.
chasseur: (hunter) a French cooking style in which meat and chicken dishes are cooked with mushrooms, shallots, white wine, and often tomato. See also cacciatora.
clarify: to melt butter and drain the oil off the sediment.
coat: to cover with a thin layer of flour, sugar, nuts, crumbs, poppy or sesame seeds, cinnamon sugar or a few of the ground spices.
concasser: to chop coarsely, usually tomatoes.
confit: from the French verb confire, meaning to preserve. Food that is made into a preserve by cooking very slowly and thoroughly until tender. In the case of meat, such as duck or goose, it is cooked in its own fat, and covered with it so that it does not come into contact with the air. Vegetables such as onions are good in confit.
consomme: a clear soup usually made from beef.
coulis: a thin puree, usually of fresh or cooked fruit or vegetables, which is soft enough to pour (couler means 'to run'). A coulis may be rough-textured or very smooth.
court bouillon: the liquid in which fish, poultry or meat is cooked. It usually consists of water with bay leaf, onion, carrots and salt and freshly ground black pepper to taste. Other additives can include wine, vinegar, stock, garlic or spring onions (scallions).
couscous: cereal processed from semolina into pellets, traditionally steamed and served with meat and vegetables in the classic North African stew of the same name.
cruciferous vegetables: certain members of the mustard, cabbage and turnip families with cross-shaped flowers and strong aromas and flavours.
cream: to make soft, smooth and creamy by rubbing with back of spoon or by beating with mixer. Usually applied to fat and sugar.
croutons: small toasted or fried cubes of bread.
crudites: raw vegetables, whether cut in slices or sticks to nibble plain or with a dipping sauce, or shredded and tossed as salad with a simple dressing.
cube: to cut into small pieces with six equal sides.
curdle: to cause milk or sauce to separate into solid and liquid. Example, overcooked egg mixtures.
daikon radish: (also called mooli): a long white Japanese radish. dark sesame oil (also called Oriental sesame oil): dark polyunsaturated oil with a low burning point, used for seasoning. Do not replace with lighter sesame oil.
deglaze: to dissolve congealed cooking juices or glaze on the bottom of a pan by adding a liquid, then scraping and stirring vigorously whilst bringing the liquid to the boil. Juices may be used to make gravy or to add to sauce.
degrease: to skim grease from the surface of liquid. If possible the liquid should be chilled so the fat solidifies. If not, skim off most of the fat with a large metal spoon, then trail strips of paper towel on the surface of the liquid to remove any remaining globules.
devilled: a dish or sauce that is highly seasoned with a hot ingredient such as mustard, Worcestershire sauce or cayenne pepper.
dice: to cut into small cubes.
dietary fibre: a plant-cell material that is undigested or only partially digested in the human body, but which promotes healthy digestion of other food matter.
dissolve: mix a dry ingredient with liquid until absorbed.
dredge: to coat with a dry ingredient, as flour or sugar.
drizzle: to pour in a fine thread-like stream over a surface.
dust: to sprinkle or coat lightly with flour or icing sugar.
Dutch oven: a heavy casserole with a lid usually made from cast iron or pottery.
emulsion: a mixture of two liquids that are not mutually soluble- for example, oil and water.
entree: in Europe, the "entry" or hors d'oeuvre; in North America entree means the main course.
fillet: special cut of beef, lamb, pork or veal; breast of poultry and game; fish cut of the bone lengthways.
flake: to break into small pieces with a fork.
flame: to ignite warmed alcohol over food.
fold in: a gentle, careful combining of a light or delicate mixture with a heavier mixture using a metal spoon.
fricassee: a dish in which poultry, fish or vegetables are bound together with a white or veloute sauce. In Britain and the United States, the name applies to an old-fashioned dish of chicken in a creamy sauce.
galette: sweet or savoury mixture shaped as a flat round.
garnish: to decorate food, usually with something edible.
gastrique: caramelized sugar deglazed with vinegar and used in fruit-flavoured savoury sauces, in such dishes as duck with orange.
glaze: a thin coating of beaten egg, syrup or aspic which is brushed over pastry, fruits or cooked meats.
gluten: a protein in flour that is developed when dough is kneaded, making it elastic.
gratin: a dish cooked in the oven or under the grill so that it develops a brown crust. Breadcrumbs or cheese may be sprinkled on top first. Shallow gratin dishes ensure a maximum area of crust.
grease: to rub or brush lightly with oil or fat.

joint: to cut poultry, game or small animals into serving pieces by dividing at the joint.
julienne: to cut food into match-like strips.
knead: to work dough using heel of hand with a pressing motion, while stretching and folding the dough.
line: to cover the inside of a container with paper, to protect or aid in removing mixture.
infuse: to immerse herbs, spices or other flavourings in hot liquid to flavour it. Infusion takes from two to five minutes depending on the flavouring. The liquid should be very hot but not boiling.
jardiniere: a garnish of garden vegetables, typically carrots, pickling onions, French beans and turnips.
lights: lungs of an animal, used in various meat preparations such as pates and faggots.
macerate: to soak food in liquid to soften.
marinade: a seasoned liquid, usually an oil and acid mixture, in which meats or other foods are soaked to soften and give more flavour.
marinara: Italian "sailor's style" cooking that does not apply to any particular combination of ingredients. Marinara tomato sauce for pasta is most familiar.
marinate: to let food stand in a marinade to season and tenderize.
mask: to cover cooked food with sauce.
melt: to heat until liquified.
mince: to grind into very small pieces.
mix: to combine ingredients by stirring.
monounsaturated fats: one of three types of fats found in foods. Are believed not to raise the level of cholesterol in the blood.
nicoise: a garnish of tomatoes, garlic and black olives; a salad with anchovy, tuna and French beans is typical.
non-reactive pan: a cooking pan whose surface does not chemically react with food. Materials used include stainless steel, enamel, glass and some alloys.
noisette: small "nut" of lamb cut from boned loin or rack that is rolled, tied and cut in neat slices. Noisette also means flavoured with hazelnuts, or butter cooked to a nut brown colour.
normande: a cooking style for fish, with a garnish of shrimp, mussels and mushrooms in a white wine cream sauce; for poultry and meat, a sauce with cream, Calvados and apple.
olive oil: various grades of oil extract from olives. Extra virgin olive oil has a full, fruity flavour and the lowest acidity. Virgin olive oil is slightly higher in acidity and lighter in flavour. Pure olive oil is a processed blend of olive oils and has the highest acidity and lightest taste.
panade: a mixture for binding stuffings and dumplings, notably quenelles, often of choux pastry or simply breadcrumbs. A panade may also be made of frangipane, pureed potatoes or rice.
papillote: to cook food in oiled or buttered greasepoof paper or aluminium foil. Also a decorative frill to cover bone ends of chops and poultry drumsticks.
parboil: to boil or simmer until part cooked (i.e. cooked further than when blanching).
pare: to cut away outside covering.
pate: a paste of meat or seafood used as a spread for toast or crackers.
paupiette: a thin slice of meat, poultry or fish spread with a savoury stuffing and rolled. In the United States this is also called "bird" and in Britain an "olive".
peel: to strip away outside covering.
plump: to soak in liquid or moisten thoroughly until full and round.
poach: to simmer gently in enough hot liquid to cover, using care to retain shape of food.
polyunsaturated fat: one of the three types of fats found in food. These exist in large quantities in such vegetable oils as safflower, sunflower, corn and soya bean. These fats lower the level of cholesterol in the blood.
puree: a smooth paste, usually of vegetables or fruits, made by putting foods through a sieve, food mill or liquefying in a blender or food processor.
ragout: traditionally a well-seasoned, rich stew containing meat, vegetables and wine. Nowadays, a term applied to any stewed mixture.
ramekins: small oval or round individual baking dishes.
reconstitute: to put moisture back into dehydrated foods by soaking in liquid.
reduce: to cook over a very high heat, uncovered, until the liquid is reduced by evaporation.
refresh: to cool hot food quickly, either under running water or by plunging it into iced water, to stop it cooking. Particularly for vegetables and occasionally for shellfish.
rice vinegar: mild, fragrant vinegar that is less sweet than cider vinegar and not as harsh as distilled malt vinegar. Japanese rice vinegar is milder than the Chinese variety.
roulade: a piece of meat, usually pork or veal, that is spread with stuffing, rolled and often braised or poached. A roulade may also be a sweet or savoury mixture that is baked in a Swiss roll tin or paper case, filled with a contrasting filling, and rolled.
rubbing-in: a method of incorporating fat into flour, by use of fingertips only. Also incorporates air into mixture.
safflower oil: the vegetable oil that contains the highest proportion of polyunsaturated fats.
salsa: a juice derived from the main ingredient being cooked or a sauce added to a dish to enhance its flavour. In Italy the term is often used for pasta sauces; in Mexico the name usually applies to uncooked sauces served as an accompaniment, especially to corn chips.
saturated fats: one of the three types of fats found in foods. These exist in large quantities in animal products, coconut and palm oils; they raise the level of cholesterol in the blood. As high cholesterol levels may cause heart disease, saturated fat consumption is recommended to be less than 15% of kilojoules provided by the daily diet.
sauté: to cook or brown in small amount of hot fat.
score: to mark food with cuts, notches of lines to prevent curling or to make food more attractive.
scald: to bring just to boiling point, usually for milk. Also to rinse with boiling water.
sear: to brown surface quickly over high heat in hot dish.
seasoned flour: flour with salt and pepper added.
sift: to shake a dry, powdered substance through a sieve or sifter to remove any lumps and give lightness.
simmer: to cook food gently in liquid that bubbles steadily just below boiling point so that the food cooks in even heat without breaking up.
singe: to quickly flame poultry to remove all traces of feathers after plucking.
skim: to remove a surface layer (often of impurities and scum) from a liquid with a metal spoon or small ladle.
slivered: sliced in long, thin pieces, usually refers to nuts, especially almonds.
soften: ie: gelatine - sprinkle over cold water and allow to gel (soften) then dissolve and liquefy.
souse: to cover food, particularly fish, in wine vinegar and spices and cook slowly; the food is cooled in the same liquid. Sousing gives food a pickled flavour.
steep: to soak in warm or cold liquid in order to soften food and draw out strong flavours or impurities.
stir-fry: to cook thin slices of meat and vegetable over a high heat in a small amount of oil, stirring constantly to even cooking in a short time. Traditionally cooked in a wok, however a heavy based frying pan may be used.
stock: a liquid containing flavours, extracts and nutrients of bones, meat, fish or vegetables.
stud: to adorn with; for example, baked ham studded with whole cloves.
sweat: to cook vegetables over heat until only juices run.
sugo: an Italian sauce made from the liquid or juice extracted from fruit or meat during cooking.
sweat: to cook sliced or chopped food, usually vegetables, in a little fat and no liquid over very low heat. Foil is pressed on top so that the food steams in its own juices, usually before being added to other dishes.
timbale: a creamy mixture of vegetables or meat baked in a mould. French for "kettledrum"; also denotes a drum-shaped baking dish.
thicken: to make a thin, smooth paste by mixing together arrowroot, cornflour or flour with an equal amount of cold water; stir into hot liquid, cook, stirring until thickened.
toss: to gently mix ingredients with two forks or fork and spoon.
total fat: the individual daily intake of all three fats previously described in this glossary. Nutritionists recommend that fats provide no more than 35% of the energy in the diet.
vine leaves: tender, lightly flavoured leaves of the grapevine, used in ethnic cuisine as wrappers for savoury mixtures. As the leaves are usually packed in brine, they should be well rinsed before use.
whip: to beat rapidly, incorporate air and produce expansion.
zest: thin outer layer of citrus fruits containing the aromatic citrus oil. It is usually thinly pared with a vegetable peeler, or grated with a zester or grater to separate it from the bitter white pith underneath.

Cooking is not an exact science: one does not require finely calibrated scales, pipettes and scientific equipment to cook, yet the conversion to metric measures in some countries and its interpretations must have intimidated many a good cook.

Weights are given in the recipes only for ingredients such as meats, fish, poultry and some vegetables. Though a few grams/ounces one way or another will not affect the success of your dish.

Though recipes have been tested using the Australian Standard 250mL cup, 20mL tablespoon and 5mL teaspoon, they will work just as well with the US and Canadian 8fl oz cup, or the UK 300mL cup. We have used graduated cup measures in preference to tablespoon measures so that proportions are always the same. Where tablespoon measures have been given, these are not crucial measures, so using the smaller tablespoon of the US or UK will not affect the recipe's success. At least we all agree on the teaspoon size.

For breads, cakes and pastries, the only area which might cause concern is where eggs are used, as proportions will then vary. If working with a 250mL or 300mL cup, use large eggs (65g/2¼oz), adding a little more liquid to the recipe for 300mL cup measures if it seems necessary. Use the medium-sized eggs (55g/2oz) with 8fl oz cup measure. A graduated set of measuring cups and spoons is recommended, the cups in particular for measuring dry ingredients. Remember to level such ingredients to ensure their accuracy.

English measures

All measurements are similar to Australian with two exceptions: the English cup measures 300mL/10½fl oz, whereas the Australian cup measure 250mL/8¾fl oz. The English tablespoon (the Australian dessertspoon) measures 14.8mL/½fl oz against the Australian tablespoon of 20mL/¾fl oz.

American measures

The American reputed pint is 16fl oz, a quart is equal to 32fl oz and the American gallon, 128fl oz. The Imperial measurement is 20fl oz to the pint, 40fl oz a quart and 160fl oz one gallon. The American tablespoon is equal to 14.8mL/½fl oz, the teaspoon is 5mL/⅙fl oz. The cup measure is 250mL/8¾fl oz, the same as Australia.

Dry measures

All the measures are level, so when you have filled a cup or spoon, level it off with the edge of a knife. The scale below is the "cook's equivalent"; it is not an exact conversion of metric to imperial measurement. To calculate the exact metric equivalent yourself, multiply ounces x 28.349523 to obtain grams, or divide 28.349523 grams to obtain ounces.

Metric	Imperial
g = grams	oz = ounces
kg = kilograms	lb = pound
15g	½oz
20g	⅔oz
30g	1oz
55g	2oz
85g	3oz
115g	4oz/¼ lb
125g	4½oz
140/145g	5oz
170g	6oz
200g	7oz
225g	8oz/½ lb
315g	11oz
340g	12oz/¾ lb
370g	13oz
400g	14oz
425g	15oz
455g	16oz/1 lb
1,000g/1kg	35.3oz/2.2 lb
1.5kg	3.3 lb

Oven temperatures

The Celsius temperatures given here are not exact; they have been rounded off and are given as a guide only. Follow the manufacturer's temperature guide, relating it to oven description given in the recipe. Remember gas ovens are hottest at the top, electric ovens at the bottom and convection-fan forced ovens are usually even throughout. We included Regulo numbers for gas cookers which may assist. To convert °C to °F multiply °C by 9 and divide by 5 then add 32.

Oven temperatures

	C°	F°	Gas regulo
Very slow	120	250	1
Slow	150	300	2
Moderately slow	160	325	3
Moderate	180	350	4
Moderately hot	190-200	370-400	5-6
Hot	210-220	410-440	6-7
Very hot	230	450	8
Super hot	250-290	475-500	9-10

Cake dish sizes

metric	imperial
15cm	6in
18cm	7in
20cm	8in
23cm	9in

Loaf dish sizes

metric	imperial
23x12cm	9x5in
25x8cm	10x3in
28x18cm	11x7in

Liquid measures

metric	imperial	cup and spoon
mL	fl oz	
millilitres	fluid ounce	
5mL	1/6fl oz	1 teaspoon
20mL	2/3fl oz	1 tablespoon
30mL	1fl oz	1 tablespoon
	plus 2 teaspoons	
55mL	2fl oz	1/4 cup
85mL	3fl oz	
115mL	4fl oz	1/2 cup
125mL	4 1/2fl oz	
150mL	5 1/4fl oz	
170mL	6fl oz	3/4 cup
225mL	8fl oz	1 cup
300mL	10 1/2fl oz	
370mL	13fl oz	
400mL	14fl oz	1 3/4 cups
455mL	16fl oz	2 cups
570mL	20fl oz	2 1/2 cups
1 litre	35.3fl oz	4 cups

Cup measurements

One cup is equal to the following weights.

	Metric	Imperial
Almonds, flaked	85g	3oz
Almonds, slivered, ground	125g	4 1/2oz
Almonds, kernel	155g	5 1/2oz
Apples, dried, chopped	125g	4 1/2oz
Apricots, dried, chopped	190g	6 3/4oz
Breadcrumbs, packet	125g	4 1/2oz
Breadcrumbs, soft	55g	2oz
Cheese, grated	115g	4oz
Choc bits	155 1/2g	5oz
Coconut, desiccated	90g	3oz
Cornflakes	30g	1oz
Currants	155 1/2g	5oz
Flour	115g	4oz
Fruit, dried (mixed, sultanas etc)	170g	6oz
Ginger, crystallised, glace	250g	8oz
Honey, treacle, golden syrup	315g	11oz
Mixed peel	225g	8oz
Nuts, chopped	115g	4oz
Prunes, chopped	225g	8oz
Rice, cooked	155g	5 1/2oz
Rice, uncooked	225g	8oz
Rolled oats	90g	3oz
Sesame seeds	115g	4oz
Shortening (butter, margarine)	225g	8oz
Sugar, brown	155g	5 1/2oz
Sugar, granulated or caster	225g	8oz
Sugar, sifted icing	155g	5 1/2oz
Wheatgerm	60g	2oz

Length

Some of us still have trouble converting imperial length to metric. In this scale, measures have been rounded off to the easiest-to-use and most acceptable figures.
To obtain the exact metric equivalent in converting inches to centimetres, multiply inches by 2.54 whereby 1 inch equals 25.4 millimetres and 1 millimetre equals 0.03937 inches.

Metric	Imperial
mm=millimetres	in = inches
cm=centimetres	ft = feet
5mm, 0.5cm	1/4in
10mm, 1.0cm	1/2in
20mm, 2.0cm	3/4in
2.5cm	1in
5cm	2in
7 1/2cm	3in
10cm	4in
12 1/2cm	5in
15cm	6in
18cm	7in
20cm	8in
23cm	9in
25cm	10in
28cm	11in
30cm	12in, 1ft

INDEX